WHEN△DISASTER△STRIKES

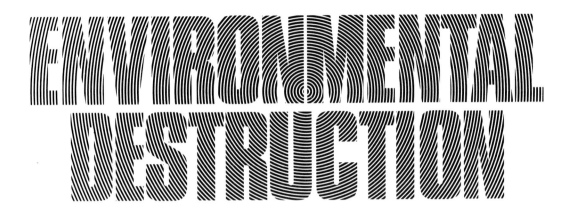

ENVIRONMENTAL DESTRUCTION

Aleksandrs Rozens

TFCB

TWENTY-FIRST CENTURY BOOKS

A Division of Henry Holt and Company
New York

Twenty-First Century Books
A division of Henry Holt and Company, Inc.
115 West 18th Street
New York, New York 10011

Henry Holt® and colophon are trademarks of Henry Holt and
Company, Inc.
Publishers since 1866

Published in Canada by Fitzhenry & Whiteside Ltd.
195 Allstate Parkway, Markham, Ontario L3R 4T8

Printed in the United States of America

All editions are printed on acid-free paper ∞.

Created and produced in association with Blackbirch Graphics, Inc.

Library of Congress Cataloging-in-Publication Data

Rozens, Aleksandrs, 1967–
    Environmental destruction / Aleksandrs Rozens. — 1st ed.
        p.   cm. — (When disaster strikes)
    Includes index.
    ISBN 0-8050-3098-0 (alk. paper)
    1. Environmental degradation—North America—Juvenile literature. 2.
Radioactive pollution—North America—Juvenile literature. 3. Oil spills—
Environmental aspects—North America—Juvenile literature. [1. Environmental
degradation. 2. Pollution. 3. Environmental protection.] I. Title. II. Series.
GE160.N7R69   1994
363.73—dc20
                                                                                93-41213
                                                                                  CIP
                                                                                  AC

Contents

Trouble with Alaska's Black Gold

In the spring of 1989, the still icy, cold waters of Prince William Sound and the surrounding land were beginning to teem with life. Birds were migrating north and bears were emerging from their winter hibernation. Otters and seals were already playing on the chunks of ice along the shore. In the deeper waters, giant whales were feeding on fish and plankton.

Opposite:
A dismayed fisherman watches as a boat alongside his pulls a dead, oil-covered bird from the water, following an oil spill in Alaska caused by the *Exxon Valdez*.

Then, on March 24, 1989, life in the Sound and for many Alaskans dramatically changed when an oil tanker ran aground and spilled its cargo.

The *Exxon Valdez*, a 987-foot-long (301-meter-long) oil tanker, had just taken on a load of oil at Port Valdez, Alaska, when it passed through the tricky Valdez Narrows. Up on the ship's bridge, Captain Joseph Hazelwood changed course to avoid any icebergs that might have drifted into the shipping lane from the Columbia Glacier that is located in one of Prince William Sound's northern bays.

Having adjusted the tanker's course, Captain Hazelwood left Gregory Cousins, the ship's third mate, in charge of the bridge. But Cousins was not licensed by the Coast Guard to pilot a tanker through the Sound's tricky waters. An important federal regulation was violated when Hazelwood gave Cousins control of the *Valdez*. The ship entered Prince William Sound and Cousins was given orders to return to the original course once the tanker reached Busby Island.

At 11:55 P.M., when the ship reached Busby Island, Cousins ordered a wrong turn. He was unable to correct his mistake—the ship was too large—and the *Valdez* sailed into an area of the Sound filled with treacherous reefs. Cousins radioed to Hazelwood, who was in his quarters,

and explained what was happening: "I think we're in serious trouble." But, it was already too late.

At four minutes past midnight, the *Exxon Valdez* struck Bligh Reef, spilling millions of gallons (liters) of its "black gold" into the Sound.

As soon as word about the disaster spread, fishermen who relied on the Sound's bounteous fish crop were angry, alarmed, and saddened. In Valdez, many fishermen wore black armbands to signify their grief, and some cried openly. Flags in several villages were lowered to half staff to mark the massive destruction that Prince William Sound had suffered.

Many environmental disasters are accidental, but others are the result of carelessness or neglect and can be avoided. Whatever the cause, the results are often the same: the disaster sites suffer extensive damage, which may last for years.

Taken immediately after the 1989 *Exxon Valdez* disaster occurred, this aerial view shows the slick that was created after oil spilled into Prince William Sound.

△ 7

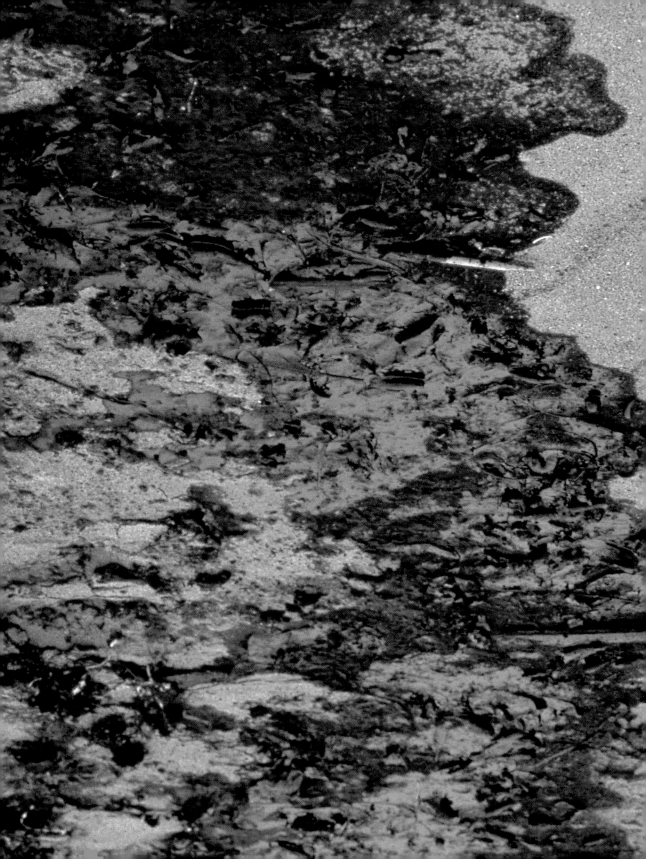

Oil Spills

The Origin of Oil Use

In 1850, Samuel Kier, a Pennsylvania resident, was the first person to drill for oil in the United States. Kier refined the oil he recovered for only one use—kerosene. He used the kerosene for fuel and burned it in kerosene lamps to produce light.

Electric lighting was not introduced in the United States until almost thirty years later. The city of Cleveland installed electric lights along its streets in 1879. Until then, people found their way in the dark with candles or kerosene lamps as their only sources of light.

Opposite:
For over one hundred years, oil spills have polluted North American waters. Here, oil-contaminated water washes onto the shores of a beach in Neah Bay, in Washington State.

The First Oil Spill

The first oil spill in North America may have taken place as early as 1818, more than thirty years before Samuel Kier ever drilled for oil. Two men digging for salt at the mouth of the Cumberland River in Kentucky had drilled a hole 536 feet (163 meters) deep, and about 5 inches (13 centimeters) wide. When oil came gushing to the surface, it began to flow into the river. Filling the hole with sand didn't stop the leak, so there was nothing to do but let the oil flow. Soon, a 35-mile (56-kilometer) stretch of the Cumberland was covered with an oil slick. And somehow, the oil on the river caught fire. Flames from the slick burned trees along the river-bank and destroyed the miners' digging facilities.

While the 1818 Cumberland River oil spill was large, it was just the beginning of a string of oil spills that have fouled our waterways.

Transporting Oil Products by Water

Many of today's oil spills have been the result of oil tankers running aground or colliding with each other. Some tankers have been crippled by storms, leaving crews helpless and unable to manage their dangerous cargo.

The first petroleum shipment to travel across water by boat took place in 1861. At that time, just 1,329 barrels of oil were shipped on the

Elizabeth Watts from Philadelphia to London, England.

The first bulk tanker that was built to transport large quantities of oil across an ocean was constructed in 1886 in England. The design of large tanks built into the hull has remained basically the same over the years; however, oil capacity has increased. The *Exxon Valdez* can carry 260,000 barrels of oil, almost 11 million gallons (42 million liters), and is 987 feet (301 meters) long.

However, oil spills do not occur only when something goes wrong with a tanker. They can also happen at offshore drilling platforms or at loading facilities.

Santa Barbara, California: 1969

Twenty years before the *Exxon Valdez* spilled its cargo off the Alaskan coastline, a different type of oil spill caught the public's attention and brought the oil industry under closer scrutiny. This spill occurred off the scenic coastline of California.

Offshore drilling along the coast had been going on for 75 years when an oil drilling platform leaked 3 million gallons (11 million liters) of oil into the waters off Santa Barbara. At the time of the leak, there were thousands of oil wells off the coast between Santa Barbara and

Los Angeles. Most of them were unregulated, which meant that oil companies did not have to abide by any safety regulations.

The leak from Union Oil Company's "Platform A" started early in the morning on January 28, 1969. A drill from the platform had cut a hole into the ocean floor in an area where there was a high pressure deposit of both oil and gas. When platform crews forced a 500-foot-long (153-meter-long) drilling pipe into the hole, the immense underground pressure pushed up the gas and oil in five different places.

Thirty men worked around the clock using various types of mud, trying to plug up the five cavities. They also used a pipeline to drain oil from the holes.

Dispersants (chemicals that break up oil) were used, but appeared to have little effect. Two Coast Guard ships helped spray the oily waters with chemicals, and crop-duster airplanes also sprayed dispersants from high above the stricken area. Cleanup crews spread talc over the slick, hoping that it would make the oil coagulate, or thicken, into large clumps that could easily be taken out of the water.

The Union Oil Company installed a special "sea curtain" on the shore side of the drilling platform to stop the spread of the slick. Plastic-filled pillows were attached to the bottom of

this stiff curtain and were sunk 3 feet (1 meter) below the water's surface, leaving a portion of the rigid material sticking up out of the water. The hope was that the oil would be swept against this barrier and be contained. Partially successful, the curtain enabled special tanker ships to retrieve some of the oil from the water's surface.

By late evening, the Coast Guard reported that most of the leaking had been halted. But the spill, and its damage, continued to spread. Twenty miles (32 kilometers) of California coastline were fouled. Hundreds of seabirds were killed by the slick. Many of these birds drowned, and others, trying to pick the oil out of their feathers, died from ingesting it.

The California Fish and Game Department began a program to pick up and clean oil-soaked birds found along the beaches. A Fish and Game Department spokesman expressed concern about shellfish that inhabited the af-fected area. The department also believed that the dispersants might threaten porpoises and the gray whales that migrate in that area.

As a result of the Santa Barbara oil spill, strict regulations were developed that make oil-spill cleanup the responsibility of the oil companies. Questions about the safety and necessity of offshore drilling were also raised. But it wasn't

WHAT IS THE EPA?

The Environmental Protection Agency (EPA) is much like an environmental police force. As part of the federal government, it was established under President Richard Nixon's administration in 1970 by the National Environmental Protection Act. The goal of this legislation was to regulate noise pollution, pesticides, toxic (poisonous) substances, and ocean dumping. The law was also part of a series of acts through which the U.S. government was trying to protect wilderness areas, endangered species, and scenic rivers.

Two important roles the EPA plays are to determine if environmental laws are being followed, and to educate the public in hope that pollution can be prevented before it has a chance to be created. The EPA is also responsible for discovering which polluted locations in the United States are in need of immediate cleanup.

Another important function of the EPA is to work together with other nations to discover, prevent, and correct pollution problems that occur worldwide.

until 1990 that the U.S. government altered its policy of leasing offshore land to oil companies.

Two years after the spill, in 1971, the Union Oil Company and three other companies paid $4.5 million to settle claims for California property that was damaged by the Santa Barbara oil spill.

Nantucket Island, Massachusetts: 1976

Nantucket Island is located off the coast of Cape Cod, an arm of Massachusetts that extends into the Atlantic Ocean. The waters around Nantucket Island not only lure summer visitors, but are also the site of one of the richest commercial fisheries along the entire Atlantic coastline of the United States.

△ 15

Waves crash over the grounded *Argo Merchant* after storm waves ripped open its hull, spilling fuel into the Atlantic Ocean in December 1976.

It was in these waters on December 15, 1976, that a 640-foot (195-meter) Liberian oil tanker, the *Argo Merchant*, ran aground on sandbars south of Nantucket Island. This was not the first time the ship's hull had scraped the ocean's bottom.

The *Argo Merchant* had a history of running off course and getting stuck in shallow water. It had grounded off the coast of Italy in 1971 for nearly sixty hours, and in September 1969, the tanker was trapped for thirty-six hours off the island of Borneo in the South Pacific.

The Coast Guard said that the ship's captain, George Papadoppoulos, was the one at fault in the Nantucket accident. "This man had all sorts of equipment he didn't use," said Coast Guard Commandant Owen W. Siler. Siler added that "it's possible to navigate much more closely than he [the ship's captain] did." One Environmental Protection Agency official estimated that Papadoppoulos had sailed his ship 10 miles (16 kilometers) off course.

Five days later, on the evening of December 20, 1976, a storm broke the *Argo Merchant* apart and 7.5 million gallons (28 million liters) of heavy industrial fuel oil gushed into the water and formed a slick about 120 miles (193 kilometers) long, causing massive damage to the New England fishing industry.

The Exxon Valdez Spill, Alaska: 1989

Alaska is very rich in oil and other natural resources. The oil industry has brought a great deal of money to the state and its people. In fact, each resident of Alaska receives an annual check from the government for his or her share of the profits that were made from oil drilled in the state. Much of the oil drilled in Alaska is transported by tankers to the rest of the United States. One of these many tankers was the *Exxon Valdez.*

On March 24, 1989, the *Exxon Valdez* struck Bligh Reef in Prince William Sound, Alaska.

When the ship struck the reef, the tanker's hull was cut open like a giant tin can. The hole was almost 18 feet (5.5 meters) wide!

Oil began gushing out of the tanker, creating a black wave that was 3 feet (1 meter) high on Prince William Sound. With the *Valdez* stuck on the reef, there remained the ominous possibility that the tanker would be further damaged by the rocks. Within several hours, 11 million gallons (42 million liters) of thick crude oil had rushed out into the waters of the Sound. The slick that was created soon spread, endangering wildlife both on land and in the water.

The damage caused by the *Exxon Valdez* spill was made even worse by the fact that the Alyeska Pipeline Service Company, which operated the trans-Alaska pipeline, was unprepared for the disaster. (Oil drilled in the northern regions of Alaska is pumped through this 800-mile-long (1,287-kilometer-long) pipeline.) The Alyeska Pipeline Service Company is run by several oil companies that drill in Alaska. Its job is to have equipment ready for use in case of a spill emergency.

However, at the time of the accident, supplies and equipment needed to contain an oil spill (to keep it from spreading) had not been

loaded onto a barge and set aside for spill cleanup duties. Some of the equipment had been left in warehouses, and important spill-control supplies were buried deep in snow.

Uncontained, the oil spill soon covered an area that was 4 miles (6 kilometers) wide in Prince William Sound.

Dispersants were not effective in controlling the spill. Cleanup crews discovered that the dispersants required choppy waters to be effective, but the Sound's waters were very calm when the chemicals were used. Some fishermen, hoping to preserve their fishing grounds, tried picking up oil out of the water with buckets.

The *Exxon Valdez* sits in Prince William Sound as other boats arrive to help contain the massive oil spill.

△ **19**

Tom Copeland and two other Valdez fishermen recovered 5,500 gallons (20,818 liters) of crude by scooping it up manually with buckets from rubber rafts. However, the size of the spill made the fishermen's efforts useless.

By March 26, just two days after the *Exxon Valdez* hit Bligh Reef, the spill covered 100 square miles (161 square kilometers) and the weather had gotten stormy. In order to mop up the mess, Exxon hired 420 shoreline clean-up workers and brought in 250 ships as well as 350,000 feet (106,750 meters) of booms (temporary floating barriers). However, these special oil-containment booms were ineffective against

The oil spill not only harmed birds and sealife, it also killed animals that lived near Prince William Sound. Many animals, like this deer, died from drinking contaminated water and eating oil-covered vegetation.

the large amounts of oil, and were broken up by heavy winds. The strong winds continued to foil attempts to drop dispersants by airplane into the Sound. A plan to burn the oil was also considered, but residents along the shoreline were worried about the dangers of petroleum smoke.

A week after the accident, the spill was still out of control. An oily slick began seeping into the Pacific Ocean, threatening important fisheries. The disaster posed an enormous danger to Alaska's fishing industry outside Prince William Sound, as well.

The inlets and coves of Alaska's coastline provide an area where fish, such as salmon, lay their eggs. These salmon provide a livelihood for many of Alaska's fishermen. But salmon fisheries were not the only ones affected by the spill. There were also herring, shrimp, and crab populations at stake. Prince William Sound alone supports $90 million worth of fisheries. As a result of the spill, fishing grounds were closed because the poisonous oil was certain to be absorbed by marine life. For fishermen, their livelihood had been dramatically disrupted. They would have to learn new ways to make a living. Jim Brown, a fisherman from Cordova, a town at the east end of Prince William Sound, was proud of Alaska's "pristine environment," and was close to tears when he saw the spill.

Seals in Prince William Sound stop for a rest at this buoy. Cleanup crew volunteers had to work to remove oil from some of the seals' fur.

An EPA administrator, William K. Reilly, said that the *Exxon Valdez* spill was a "disaster of enormous impact on the environment." Jay Hair, president of the National Wildlife Federation, noted that "it's probably fair to say that in our lifetime we will never see the Sound the way it was on March 23, 1989."

The spill threatened more than the Alaskan fisheries. An entire ecosystem (a complex community of organisms in their natural environment) was soaked by record amounts of oil.

The *Exxon Valdez's* black cargo covered all the beaches of Prince William Sound. Nancy Lethcoe, a charter boat operator, feared that "they are not going to be able to clean up Prince William Sound. There is oil sinking in among the rocks at hundreds of beaches." Indeed, when the volunteers and cleanup crews arrived, they found that the oil had taken its toll on the seabirds and otters that make the sound their home. On one island, 500 dead birds were found. According to the National Wildlife Service, the spill claimed the lives of 270,000 birds. The oil had saturated the animals' feathers, and they could not fly or float. Plants that were soaked with oil poisoned the birds and other sealife that ate this vegetation. With the entire food chain endangered, Prince William Sound could not support life.

Biologists estimate that between 500 and 1,000 otters were also killed by the oil spill. The oil, which penetrated their fur, took away the otters' ability to insulate themselves from the very cold temperatures of the Sound. Many people from around the world who witnessed the plight of Alaskan wildlife came to help. Animals that had been drenched in oil were cleaned in a long process by volunteers who used toothbrushes to clean feathers and fur. The cleanup efforts continued for several months.

The long-term effect that the spill will have on Prince William Sound and the surrounding area will not be known until the environment is able to regenerate, return to its natural state, and once again sustain life. The question that many Alaskans are asking is: How much wildlife will return?

Today, the captain of the *Exxon Valdez* lives in the state of New York where he teaches at the New York Maritime College. He was sentenced by a criminal court judge in Alaska to fulfill 1,000 hours of community service in the cleanup efforts. In October 1991, the Exxon Corporation agreed to pay the state of Alaska $1 billion in fines over ten years. Although the company spent more than $2.5 billion in cleanup efforts, as much as 60 percent of the spilled oil was never recovered.

As a result of the spill, stricter regulations governing the oil industry's operations have been passed by the Alaskan government. Penalties for spills have been greatly increased, and safety measures for oil tankers have been made much more rigorous. There are also new laws that seek to improve and speed up an oil company's response to a spill. In addition, regulations for the entire oil industry are currently being re-evaluated by lawmakers in Washington, D.C.

Opposite:
A member of a cleanup crew assesses the damage from the *Exxon Valdez* spill.

Captain Joseph Hazelwood.

New York, New York: 1990

Spills along New York City's waterfront are not a new problem. About 16 billion gallons (61 billion liters) of oil products are delivered into New York Harbor each year. But, in 1990, the oil spills in New York Harbor became frequent. That year, five spills dumped a total of 1 million gallons (4 million liters) of oil into the water. Three of the spills were in narrow waterways known as the Arthur Kill and the Kill Van Kull. These waterways separate Staten Island from New Jersey. About 75 percent of the oil that is shipped through New York Harbor annually travels through the Arthur Kill.

The first spill of the year occurred on January 2, 1990. It was caused by a leaking Exxon pipeline. The leak detection system had failed and 567,000 gallons (2 million liters) of fuel gushed into the Arthur Kill. Exxon rapidly sent a cleanup crew of 170 people to the site and the 10-mile (16-kilometer) slick was contained by oil booms. Special vacuum trucks on the shoreline helped remove the oil. Charges were brought against Exxon, and $15 million was to be paid to New Jersey, New York, and the federal government, to settle civil lawsuits.

On February 28, a barge leaked 24,000 gallons (90,840 liters) of oil into the Kill Van Kull, and on March 1, another barge leaked 3,500

In June 1990, workers in small boats collected floating chunks of oil in the Kill Van Kull and deposited them on docks to be disposed of later.

gallons (13,248 liters) of heavy crude oil there. A third barge exploded on March 6, and the fire caused 200,000 gallons (757,000 liters) of heating oil to spill into the Kill Van Kull. Then, on June 7, a British tanker ran aground, empty-ing 260,000 gallons (984,100 liters) of heating oil into the troubled waters of the Kill Van Kull.

Even though New York Harbor had been heavily industrialized, biologists hoped that some wildlife might be able to live in the harbor's waters. These five spills, however, effectively erased those hopes. Wetlands where birds could nest or find food were spoiled by the vast quan-tities of oil. Instead, the blackened carcasses of ducks and gulls washed up on New York and New Jersey shores for weeks afterward.

CHAPTER 3

Radiation and Chemical Disasters

During World War II, the United States and its allies were in a desperate race against Germany to develop an atomic bomb. Both sides knew that whoever developed a nuclear weapon first would have a decisive advantage that could affect the outcome of the war.

The Manhattan Project

In the United States, the program to develop the atomic bomb, known as the Manhattan Project, took place in three areas, one of which was Hanford, Washington. There, at a special site on the Columbia River that was spread out over

Opposite:
An atomic bomb is detonated during a test in the Nevada desert in 1955.

570 square miles (917 square kilometers), a group of scientists produced plutonium, a dangerously radioactive substance, for what would be the first atomic bomb.

The U.S. government established the Hanford Atomic Works in 1944 and hired E.I. Du Pont de Nemours, Inc., as the prime contractor for the site. In 1946, the General Electric Company took Du Pont's place as prime contractor.

The atomic reactors needed to manufacture the plutonium were built by the U.S. Army Corps of Engineers. The Hanford site had eight reactors that could produce plutonium.

Until 1971, when the last reactor closed, the Hanford plant produced 50 tons (45 metric tons) of plutonium. Through the years, many plant workers were exposed to high levels of radiation. Little was done to protect them.

While the plant's managers and the U.S. government were aware of the dangerously high levels of radiation that Hanford plant workers were being exposed to, the importance of constructing an atomic bomb kept people quiet. But finally, in February 1986, special documents detailing the plant's radiation accidents were released to the public. An environmental group, the Hanford Education Action League, had filed a request with the Department of Energy under the Freedom of Information Act.

Dr. J.R. Oppenheimer (right) directed the Manhattan Project during the 1940s.

According to these documents, experimental military testing of the bomb prototype (a first model) released a radioactive cloud that covered 800 square miles (1,287 square kilometers). This cloud contaminated crops and fields where cattle grazed in parts of Washington, Oregon, and Montana.

The Columbia River was contaminated by radiation as well. When all eight reactors were producing plutonium, enormous amounts of iodine (an element that is also a waste product of plutonium production) were also being dumped directly into the river, causing significant contamination.

After the reactors were shut down, the plant itself continued to operate, and much of the plutonium that had been created was still on site.

△ **31**

On August 30, 1976, the Hanford plant had one of its most serious radiation accidents when it was rocked by an explosion. A plant worker, Harold McCluskey, was exposed to huge amounts of radiation, and was badly burned by bits and pieces of flying radioactive metals and glass. He also inhaled irradiated air. Nine other workers were injured as well, but none were exposed to as much radiation as McCluskey, who needed special treatments to counteract the radiation.

A Hanford plant worker guards a contaminated area after an explosion in 1976. Ten workers were exposed to radiation during this accident.

The experiments at Hanford had a long-term negative effect on the natural environment.

Radioactive elements were released into the air as plant operators carried out their work. Cities as far as 70 miles (113 kilometers) away experienced the effects of the dangerous levels of iodine, and there has been a high incidence of thyroid disease found in connection with this site. As many as 20,000 children (who are very susceptible to the danger of radioactive iodine) may have consumed milk produced by contaminated cows that grazed near Hanford.

Chalk River, Ontario, Canada: 1952

The world's first major nuclear reactor disaster occurred at an experimental reactor on the Chalk River, about 100 miles (161 kilometers) from the Canadian capital city of Ottawa.

The Chalk River reactor was being tested on December 12, 1952, when, through a combination of errors, it was allowed to overheat. Water, used as a coolant, leaked into the plant's basement. Luckily, everyone had evacuated the building that housed the reactor in time and no one was injured. It is not known how much radiation was released.

The Chalk River plant had a second accident in 1958. Radioactive fuel leaked into a reactor tank and remained unnoticed until the reactor overheated and water from the reactor tank was dumped on the burning reactor to quench the fire. As many as 600 of the plant's personnel had to wear protective clothing while cleaning up the radioactive mess.

Full details of both Chalk River accidents were never entirely revealed, but reports suggest that both incidents definitely resulted in environmental damage.

Times Beach, Missouri: 1971

Times Beach was a community with just over 2,000 people in 1971. It was still rural and many of its roads were unpaved. Because cars and trucks would kick up dust when they drove through the area, the town had many of its

Many homes were abandoned by the residents of Times Beach, Missouri, who left because the area was contaminated with dioxin.

Workers, wearing protective gear, examine the soil in Times Beach, Missouri, in 1971.

roads coated with a special oil to reduce the amount of dust. Russell Bliss, a waste hauler, sprayed the oil throughout Times Beach. But unknown to Bliss, or to Times Beach residents, was the fact that the oil was tainted with a dangerous poison called dioxin.

Dioxin is a toxic chemical that is found in Agent Orange, a defoliant (a chemical spray used to strip plants of their leaves) used by U.S. troops during the Vietnam War. Agent Orange had been manufactured near Times Beach and had somehow seeped into the oil. The oil and its potential danger went unnoticed until eleven years later.

△ **35**

During the years after the oil was sprayed, many horses, cats, birds, and mice were found dead in Times Beach. At one point, 97 horses had died from mysterious causes. The horses had been kept in stables not far from where the dioxin-tainted oil had been sprayed.

In 1985, when Times Beach was evacuated, 58 families refused to leave. Most of the town, however, did leave, including the town's police force. The U.S. government spent $33 million to actually buy the town so it could be cleaned. Another $480 million was spent by the federal government to incinerate the dioxin-contaminated dirt. The plan to incinerate the dirt was criticized because people feared dioxin would then contaminate the air. A Missouri court judge finally approved the incineration plan.

After the incineration plan was approved, and against the wishes of the Red Cross, 200 families went back to retrieve belongings left behind during the evacuation. The remaining families left and Times Beach was abandoned. The community quickly became a ghost town. A barricade stood at the entrance to the town displaying a sign that read: "Keep Out." Below the sign was a picture of a skull and crossbones—the international symbol for poison—a symbol that former residents of Times Beach knew well.

Three Mile Island, Pennsylvania: 1979

On Wednesday, March 28, 1979, a nuclear power plant on the Susquehanna River, 3 miles (5 kilometers) from Harrisburg, Pennsylvania, released above-normal levels of radiation. The plant had suffered a partial core meltdown. (A meltdown occurs when the radioactive material

Two cooling towers at Three Mile Island emit steam. The 1979 meltdown at this nuclear power plant caused many families to evacuate the area.

THE DANGER OF RADIATION

Nuclear power plants are much like steam kettles. Instead of being heated by gas or electricity, though, reactors are heated by the energy created from nuclear fission—the process of splitting atoms. Fission creates both high-level and low-level radioactive wastes. Low-level wastes are found in the steam produced by the heat, but it is high-level wastes plant operators have to be most careful with. Some waste materials that result from nuclear fission can be re-used, others have to be removed and stored properly.

Radioactive materials are extremely dangerous because they kill human and animal cells—the basic building blocks of life. Radiation can damage a cell to the point that it cannot reproduce. Sometimes, radiation can mutate cells and even cause cancer. The complete range of hazardous effects from radiation is not known. It has been determined, however, that radiation does affect fertility. It can damage ovaries or testes, which may bring about sterility or an abnormal birth.

in the core of a reactor loses cooling water that regulates the core temperature.) A combination of human error and faulty equipment caused the reactor to overheat. Water in the cooling system was cut off and, as a result, uranium pellets in the fuel rods melted and cracked, releasing radiation. Four employees received an overdose of radiation and required medical treatment, and radioactive steam escaped into the air.

Initially, John Herbein, a vice president of the company that ran the power plant, suggested that the breakdown was a "minor fuel failure." But news reports continued to focus on the power plant.

Nearby residents were unsure what to do until March 30, when Pennsylvania's Governor Dick Thornburgh ordered the evacuation of children and pregnant women. People panicked, looking for ways to escape exposure to fallout (particles of radioactive material that are scattered through the atmosphere by the wind).

Families then began to leave the immediate area of Three Mile Island. National Guard members helped in the evacuation, along with state troopers, who had the responsibility of protecting evacuated areas from looters. Guardsmen and troopers wore protective lead clothing. The government also had 80 tons (73 metric tons) of lead shielding trucked to the plant in an attempt to contain the contamination.

Overhead, helicopters hovered in the area around the plant with monitoring devices to sample the air directly above the reactor. Radiation is invisible, but monitoring systems are able to track its levels. One member of the Pennsylvania Department of Environmental Resources believed that there was even more radiation in the air at Three Mile Island than there had been after a nuclear bomb test in China. Officials also watched a grid of monitoring devices that tracked radiation at ground levels. These devices had been installed throughout the Pennsylvania countryside.

Some residents decided to stay despite the mass evacuation efforts. Ed Drayer, who lived near the plant, was not worried about the trouble. His daughter, however, had to postpone her wedding reception. The American Legion Hall, where she had planned to have her reception, had been converted to an emergency press facility.

Out on the Lytle farm, where you can see the Three Mile Island cooling towers, the Lytle family could do nothing to help their cows. There was no way of moving the herd of 180 to pastures outside the immediate area.

"If those cows start leaving town on their own, I'm getting out of here, too," Clarence Lytle II joked with a newspaperman.

Many families locked up their homes and went to nearby Lancaster, York, or Gettysburg— all about 30 miles (48 kilometers) away—to stay with friends until the crisis at the plant was resolved. But some residents chose to remain. "People seem to have gotten use to it [the situation] a little," said Walter Branch, a Middletown service station operator. "Yesterday [March 30] I pumped more gas than I've ever pumped in four years. Today it's about back to normal."

By April 10, Governor Thornburgh declared that the danger was past and families could begin to return to the Three Mile Island area.

SHASTA LAKE, CALIFORNIA: 1991

On July 14, 1991, a railway car that was carrying pesticides derailed and fell into the Sacramento River in California. During the accident, the tanker car was ripped open and its lethal contents spilled out into the river. A chemical slick, nearly 1 mile (2 kilometers) long, was washed down the river, killing every living thing in the water. Three days later, the slick made its way into Shasta Lake, which serves as California's largest reservoir, and contaminated the water supply.

The Shasta Lake spill brought about the complete evacuation of the community of Dunsmuir, California. The pesticides also contaminated the air throughout this region. Residents of the area were treated for rashes, eye irritation, and headaches from the chemical spill. Some even had problems breathing. Future health problems may arise from this spill. The extent of long-term damage that can be caused by exposure to these chemicals is unknown.

With all the attention focused on the Three Mile Island accident, and on the disaster it could have been, people across the country started voicing strong doubts about the safety of, and the need for, nuclear power. President Jimmy Carter suggested that the Three Mile Island accident would "make us reassess our present safety precautions." Just how much radiation was released remains unknown. But plant operators and federal and state regulators, such as the Nuclear Regulatory Commission, said the radiation levels released were "negligible." However, incidents of cancer within the area of the plant did increase over the ten year period following the accident.

The Dangers of Waste Materials

Wastes that were improperly disposed of have often come back to haunt us. The Environmental Protection Agency estimates that there are thousands of hazardous waste sites throughout the United States alone that pose a severe threat to human health and require cleanup.

Hudson River, New York: 1946-1971

Polychlorinated Biphenyls—or PCBs as they are best known—are chemicals used in paints and insulation. They also serve as an important component of electrical transformers. But PCBs

Opposite:
These bags of toxic waste were illegally dumped in December 1990. Toxic waste management officials had to decide how to dispose of them.

are harmful in certain forms because they are toxic and carcinogenic (cancer causing).

From 1946 to 1971, two electrical plants in New York State dumped as much as 630,000 pounds (286,000 kilograms) of PCB-contaminated waste directly into the Hudson River at Fort Edward and Hudson Falls. It wasn't long before these toxic chemicals, resting on the river's bottom, began to contaminate the food chain. As a result, commercial fishing of striped bass in the river was discontinued and human consumption of other fish was also banned.

General Electric, the company responsible for the toxic dumping, paid New York State a $3

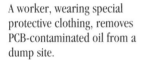
A worker, wearing special protective clothing, removes PCB-contaminated oil from a dump site.

million fine, but refuses to pay any additional money to fund cleanup efforts. The company is calling for a further study of the situation before it will agree to help with the cleanup process.

Love Canal, New York: 1978

Love Canal, a dump site located in northern New York, is near the Canadian border. For eleven years, the Hooker Chemical and Plastics Corporation carelessly dumped over 20,000 tons (18,140 metric tons) of highly toxic chemical waste in Love Canal. Then, in 1953, the company donated the site to the community's school district. The 99th Street School, as well as 100 homes, now stand in this area.

Initially, little thought was given to the chemical wastes left in Love Canal, New York, as homes and a school were constructed there. But soon, residents began noticing chemical sludge oozing through their basements. In addition, the community appeared to suffer a greater-than-normal number of birth defects. Lois Eisner, whose home was right on the edge of the canal dump site, had two miscarriages, and gave birth to a child who had a birth defect. Lois and her husband became frantic about their family. "Right now we don't know what we're going to do. My husband's parents live down the street, so we can't go there."

In 1976, Environmental Commissioner Ogden Reid ordered a ban against fishing in the Hudson River due to the toxic levels of PCBs found there.

An aerial view of Love Canal, New York.

Bonnie Snyder, who also lived near Love Canal, worried about her daughters. Snyder said, "If we can get some money, we'll move out."

It was not until 1978 that New York State officially recognized the apparent dangers related to the Love Canal site, and decided to evacuate the 240 families that lived there. As many as 500 homes were eventually evacuated. Fleets of buses took the displaced residents to a nearby air force base. Those homes located closest to the canal were destroyed. The people who lost their homes were reimbursed by both the Hooker Chemical and Plastics Corporation and the U.S. government.

When the Love Canal community was abandoned, cleanup crews sealed off the area with a chain-link fence and warning signs: "Danger

Hazardous Waste. Unauthorized Personnel Keep Out." The Love Canal site drew curiosity seekers who came to get a better look.

The government's cleanup efforts at the Love Canal site lasted from 1980 to 1990. Construction workers wearing gas masks tore down some homes, while the dump site was covered with clay that acted as a sealant. In 1990, the Environmental Protection Agency declared Love Canal safe, and homes left standing were put up for sale. The name of the community was changed to Black Creek Village and almost one-third of the homes have been sold.

WHAT IS THE SUPERFUND?

In 1980, the U.S. government passed the Comprehensive Environmental Response, Compensation, and Liability Act. This legislation set aside money in a "Superfund" for the Environmental Protection Agency's cleanup of hazardous waste dump sites. The original budget was $1.6 billion, but by 1985 it was increased to $8.5 billion with the Superfunds Amendments and Reauthorization Act.

Some of this money comes from taxes on U.S. refined or imported oil, and some from taxes on profits made by licensed hazardous waste dumps.

Sites to be cleaned up with the Superfund money are listed on what is known as the National Priorities List, which is created by the EPA. Priorities are assigned after studies of particular sites are completed. These studies include the analysis of types and quantities of waste, and the threat to human health and the surrounding environment.

A schedule for cleanup of these sites is also part of the list. Of the 1,275 sites singled out on the National Priorities List, only about 60 have been cleaned so far. The fund is still in existence today, and the number of Superfund sites on the list is expected to reach 4,000 soon. Costs for the cleanup of these sites, according to some estimates, may reach as high as $700 billion.

Medical Waste on Beaches, New Jersey, New York, and Connecticut: 1988

The Atlantic Ocean waters along the coasts of New York, New Jersey, and Connecticut have been subject to many different kinds of dumping. One of the most serious waste disposal episodes occurred in 1988, when previously used syringes and other medical supplies washed up on public beaches. This event sparked a panic that led to the closing of New York, New Jersey, and Connecticut beaches that summer. Much of the scare was prompted by fears that the syringes could be contaminated with the HIV virus (the virus that causes AIDS). The medical waste dumping was curbed largely through stepped-up policing efforts by local governments—those caught dumping faced heavy fines.

Medical waste, such as these syringes, washed up on some public beaches in New York, New Jersey, and Connecticut during the summer of 1988.

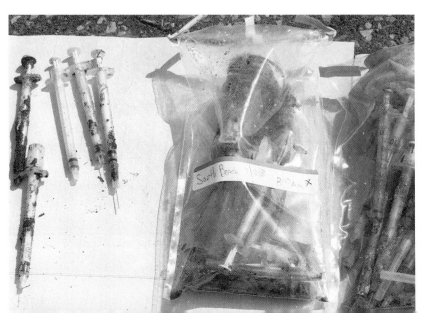

PROFITING FROM NUCLEAR WASTE

Since the early 1980s, the U.S. Department of Energy (DOE) has been searching for temporary waste disposal sites to store high-level, radioactive waste until a permanent site in Yucca Mountain, Nevada, is established. This site may not be constructed until the year 2010. Because such a facility needs to be in a sparsely populated area and accessible by major highways, some Native American tribes have considered offering portions of their land that meet these requirements.

Native American tribes who live on large reservations may be able to profit greatly from having waste sites on their land. In addition to being paid for the use of their property, the construction of the sites would provide jobs, and future aid promised by the government as part of the deal would pay for housing, roads, clinics, and other needs.

Seeking a way to support their 3,400 member tribe, the Mescalero Apaches of New Mexico are one tribe that is considering storing nuclear waste on their reservation. Tribal members who are in favor of a waste disposal site believe that the money earned would provide jobs and help alleviate housing shortages. Those who oppose the site are afraid that an accident would destroy their land. One tribal member objects to the project and said, "We were given this land by the Great Spirit. The ground we walk on is the same ground our forefathers walked upon."

Just outside the reservation, neighbors fear that a nuclear waste facility would scare away tourists and destroy the local economy. In nearby Ruidoso, New Mexico, a city council member named E. Frank Potter said, "Western tourism and nuclear storage don't mix." Both New Mexico's governor and its congressmen also oppose the idea. They successfully stopped the financing of a federal grant to the Mescaleros in October 1993 that would have enabled them to finalize a deal with the government. However, the Mescalero Apaches continue their quest that would allow them to profit from the disposal of nuclear waste.

Nuclear Wastes in the USA

One of the most dangerous types of waste is created by nuclear power plants. Radioactive uranium waste, which is released in the fission process and is most often in liquid form, has been known to leak into the air, water, and ground, where it has a long half-life (time it takes for radioactive material to break down into half the original amount).

△ **49**

Some nuclear plants have secretly leaked waste into the environment for years, poisoning and disrupting food chains. Two such plants are the Hanford Nuclear Reservation in Washington State, and the Savannah River nuclear plant in South Carolina, which produced radioactive plutonium for weapons and allowed waste to seep into nearby land and water.

Rocky Flats, Colorado: 1988

Located near Denver, Colorado, the Rocky Flats nuclear plant produced plutonium for nuclear weaponry in the 1980s. Attention was first focused on Rocky Flats in September 1988, when two plant personnel accidentally inhaled radioactive particles after wandering into an area that was contaminated. A warning sign had been obscured, so the two had no idea that the area was dangerous and off limits. A few days after this incident, the Department of Energy, which is in charge of U.S. energy policy, investigated and discovered that misplaced warning signs were not the only problem at Rocky Flats.

There had been several safety violations by plant personnel. There were also electrical problems at the plant, and a lack of sufficient radiation monitoring. The Department of Energy shut parts of the Rocky Flats plant down, citing only one contamination incident.

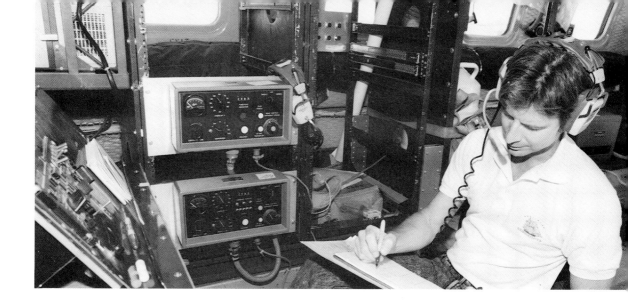

One of the main concerns surrounding the Rocky Flats plant has been the question of nuclear waste. A facility in Idaho was used as a disposal point for the plant's waste, but the governor of Idaho put a halt to the deliveries because of the contamination problem the waste might cause. The Idaho governor, however, came under pressure from the U.S. government, which said if the Idaho waste-disposal facility would not accept their deliveries, the Rocky Flats plant would have to close as well. Government officials said that this would endanger national security, so a temporary arrangement was set up to allow the plant to continue shipping its waste to Idaho.

The question of what to do with the nuclear waste still remains largely unresolved. In the meantime, however, the Rocky Flats plant continues to produce wastes that can potentially endanger the health and safety of thousands.

A plant worker fills out a log book while making a survey of the Rocky Flats plant from an airplane overhead.

△ **51**

C H A P T E R

What Can Be Done?

Dr. Maureen Y. Lichtveld, chief biomedical officer at the Agency for Toxic Substances and Disease Registry, estimates that 275 million tons (250 million metric tons) of hazardous waste are generated in the United States every year. And about 41 million U.S. residents, Lichtveld says, live within 4 miles (6 kilometers) of hazardous waste sites and may be at risk of exposure.

How Can This Problem Be Addressed?

Currently there are 64,000 hazardous waste sites in the United States that will require some level of cleanup. Only 1,358 of them have been

Opposite:
An Environmental Protection Agency employee removes toxic waste from a dump in Houston, Texas, in 1985.

CLEANING UP A SUPERFUND SITE

In order for the EPA to be able to discover and inspect a dump site that needs attention, several steps need to take place. Often, a waste site is reported to the EPA's National Response Center.

Then the EPA assembles information about the dump site using state records and geological survey maps. The EPA tries to find the party responsible for the dumping and attempts to identify the waste being disposed so it can decide just how badly the environment in a given area will be affected. Will the water table be contaminated? Is the area readily accessible to children?

EPA agents also need to determine if the site requires long-term cleanup. If so, it is then placed on the National Priorities List. This is determined by how toxic the site is, and how many people stand to be affected by it.

An extensive study is then done of the site using laboratory analysis and testing. This information helps the EPA decide how best to clean up the waste.

When the study is completed, a plan for the cleanup is developed, and it is outlined in the EPA's Record of Decision.

If you spot a dump site, call: 800-424-8802.

examined by the Agency for Toxic Substances and Disease Registry. In addition, there are tens of thousands of sites still undiscovered. A 1986 U.S. federal law provides that any state that cannot certify that it has made provisions for handling its projected hazardous waste over the next twenty years will lose millions of dollars in government funding.

During the 1990s, the Clean Water Act is expected to be changed by the U.S. government in order to help step up its efforts to control water pollution. Pesticides used in farming will be one of the issues that the government will try to address; much of today's water pollution is brought about by pesticides seeping into fresh water.

The debate over ocean dumping will also continue for many years. Some scientists believe that deep ocean dumping of sludge is not a major problem. But others argue that the dumping is sure to disrupt sea life.

One idea brought forth by those who favor deep ocean waste disposal is to dump drums of waste into the ocean floor. These heavy drums would have a special "nose cone" that would weigh the drums down and allow them to sink deep into the ocean floor.

PESTICIDES

Farmers have traditionally used pesticides to protect their crops from insects. Some of the earliest pesticides were tobacco leaves, which would naturally kill off insects. Today, however, many of the pesticides used in the battle against insects are human-made chemicals.

Certain pesticides have proven to be harmful to farm workers. In 1989, the World Health Organization estimated that pesticides poison nearly 3 million people each year. Of these 3 million, 1 in 14 dies from the exposure. While the poisoning of farm workers has occurred more often in poorer countries, U.S. farm workers have also suffered from exposure.

One toxic variety of pesticide has been known to both impair breathing and severely damage the digestive system. Other pesticides have been suspected of causing birth defects and some types of cancer. Farmers exposed to certain pesticides have had higher-than-normal incidences of lip, skin, stomach, and brain cancer.

A type of pesticide—DDT, or dicloro-diphenol-trebloroethane—introduced in the 1970s, is lethal to fish populations in the streams, creeks, or waterways near farm areas. Pesticides in the soil run off into waterways. Some bird species have been affected by pesticides because the fish populations, a major source of food for birds, have declined. Pesticides also upset the food chain by changing the natural balance of organisms in a particular area.

The Valdez Principles

As a result of the *Exxon Valdez* spill, a group of investors and environmentalists met in September 1989, and developed a code of conduct for businesses. With this code, businesses would assess what impact they have on the environment and the community in a particular area. Businesses that sign the Valdez Principles agree to:

- Eliminate pollution from their production processes.
- Produce environmentally safe products.
- Minimize production of hazardous waste.
- Dispose of hazardous waste safely.
- Use energy-efficient processes.
- Produce more energy-efficient products.
- Use renewable resources.
- Conserve non-renewable resources.
- Contribute to the preservation of biological diversity.
- Report any environmental accidents.
- Assume financial responsibility for the restoration of any damaged environment.
- Financially compensate victims of any accident attributed to their business.
- Employ an environmental affairs senior executive who will oversee adherence to the principles.
- Conduct an annual environmental audit of operations.

Safety Measures

Under the 1990 U.S. Oil Pollution Act, tankers operating in U.S. waters must have double hulls that reduce the amount of oil leakage in the event of damage to the ship. In fact, nations around the world are currently working to put

Soil samples are taken at a toxic waste site to monitor safety levels.

an agreement into effect that would require all new supertankers to be built with double hulls. Some oil tankers would be specially designed with subdivided oil containers. With subdivided containers, the amount of oil that would escape from a punctured vessel would be lessened, as in double-hulled ships.

While much political attention has been focused on the environment in recent years, there is still much more work left to be done. Many companies still believe it is easier and cheaper not to take precautions against polluting the environment. But in the long term, it is more effective for them to comply with regulations set by the EPA and its counterparts in other countries. By following strict standards, many disasters—like several of those mentioned in this book—can be prevented.

Unfortunately, it often takes an enormous disaster to draw the public's attention to short-comings in the way industries endanger our environment. If the impact of human actions on the environment is carefully considered on a regular basis, it will ensure that future generations will have a safe and clean world to enjoy. If we do not take action now to preserve the natural environment, we may ruin our chances of having a decent world for the generations still to come.

△ **59**

Glossary

boom A temporary floating barrier.

carcinogen Any substance capable of causing, or helping to cause, cancer.

defoliant A chemical used to strip plants of their leaves.

dispersants Chemicals used to dilute, or break up, a pollutant.

ecosystem A complex community of organisms in their natural environment.

fallout Particles of radioactive material that are scattered through the atmosphere after a nuclear accident.

fission The splitting of an atom. Fission is accompanied by the release of huge amounts of energy.

food chain A sequence of living things in which each organism in the community feeds upon the one below it.

half-life The time it takes for any amount of a radioactive element to decay to half the original amount.

iodine An element of the halogen group, it is also a waste product of plutonium production.

irradiate To expose to, or treat with, radiation.

nuclear reactor A device in which a nuclear reaction can be begun, continued, and controlled, in order to produce energy.

pesticide A substance, usually chemical, used to destroy harmful animals or plants.

plutonium An artificially produced radioactive element used in the production of nuclear weapons.

Polychlorinated Biphenyls (PCBs) Chemicals that are used in paint, insulation, and electrical transformers. PCBs can be harmful under certain conditions.

Further Reading

Amdur, Richard. *Toxic Materials.* New York: Chelsea House, 1993.

Bailey, Donna. *What We Can Do About Protecting Nature.* New York: Franklin Watts, 1992.

Blashfield, Jean and Black, Wallace. *Oil Spills.* Chicago, IL: Childrens Press, 1991.

Duggleby, John. *Pesticides.* New York: Crestwood House, 1990.

Galperin, Anne L. *Nuclear Energy–Nuclear Waste.* New York: Chelsea House, 1992.

Gosnell, Kevin. *Nuclear Power Stations.* New York: Franklin Watts, 1992.

Hare, Tony. *Nuclear Waste Disposal.* New York: Franklin Watts, 1991.

_____. *Toxic Waste.* New York: Franklin Watts, 1991.

Markham, Adam. *The Environment.* Vero Beach, FL: Rourke, 1988.

Source Notes

Cowley, Geoffrey. "Dead Otters, Silent Ducks," *Newsweek,* April 24, 1989.

Cross, Michael and Mick Hammer. "How to Seal a Super- tanker," *New Scientist,* March 14, 1992.

Dionne, EJ, Jr. "State Drafts Plan to Rid the Hudson of PCB 'Hot Spots,'" *The New York Times,* June 28, 1978.

Egan, Timothy. "High Winds Hamper Oil Spill Off Alaska," *The New York Times,* March 27, 1989.

Franck, Irene and David Brownstone. *The Green Encyclopedia.* New York: Prentice Hall, 1992.

Goodstein, Laurie. "Exxon Criticized Over Pipeline Spill," *The Washington Post,* January 5, 1990.

Kihss, Peter. "Oil From a Sunken Barge Closes Coney Island and Other Beaches," *The New York Times,* August 24, 1978.

Lenonick, Michael. "The Two Alaskas," *The New York Times,* April 17, 1989.

May, John. *The Greenpeace Book of the Nuclear Age: The Hidden History, The Human Cost.* New York: Pantheon, 1989.

Shabecoff, Philip. "Largest Tanker Spill Spews 270,000 Barrels of Oil Off Alaska," *The New York Times,* March 25, 1989.

Sullivan, Allanna. "Oil Spill Occurs at Exxon Dock," *Wall Street Journal,* July 19, 1990.

Toufexis, Anatasia. "Dining With Invisible Danger," *Time,* March 27, 1989.

Index

△ **63**

Acknowledgements and Photo Credits
Cover: Hodson-Greenpeace-FSP/Gamma-Liaison; pp. 4, 20, 22: ©Anchorage Daily News/Gamma-Liaison; pp. 7, 19: ©Michelle Barnes/Gamma-Liaison; p. 8: P. Dwyer/Liaison USA; pp. 13, 16, 35: Bettmann; p. 24: ©James D. Wilson/Newsweek/Gamma-Liaison; pp. 25, 28: Wide World Photos, Inc.; pp. 27, 45, 51: UPI/Bettmann; pp. 31, 32: AP/Wide World Photos; p. 34: Photo Researchers, Inc.; p. 37: ©Rose M. Prouser/Gamma-Liaison; p. 42: ©Mel Evans/Gamma-Liaison; p. 44: ©Seth Resnick/Liaison International; p. 46: United Press International; p. 48: UPI/Bettmann Newsphotos; p. 52: ©Sam C. Pierson, Jr./Photo Researchers, Inc.; p. 57: ©Paul Howell/Gamma-Liaison; p. 58: Blackbirch Press, Inc.